Animate Objects

Animate Objects

Alan R. Wilson

Turnstone Press

Turnstone Press
607–100 Arthur Street
Winnipeg, Manitoba
Canada R3B 1H3

Turnstone Press gratefully acknowledges the assistance of the Canada Council and the Manitoba Arts Council.

Some of the poems first appeared in *The Antigonish Review, Canadian Literature, The Dalhousie Review, Dandelion, The Fiddlehead, Fireweed* (as Anna Wollis), *The Malahat Review,* and *Prism International.* "Thirteen Ways of Looking at Pepper" has been included in the British Columbia Creative Writing Grade 12 Distance Learning Course. Some poems from *Animate Objects* were in the finals of the 1993 and 1994 CBC/Saturday Night Literary Awards Competition.

Cover photograph: Alan R. Wilson

Design: Manuela Dias

This book was printed and bound in Canada by Friesen Printers for Turnstone Press.

Canadian Cataloguing in Publication Data

Wilson, Alan R. (Alan Robert)

Animate objects

Poems.
ISBN 0-88801-192-X

I. Title.

PS 8595.I57A755 1995 C811'.54 C 95-920025-8
PR 9199.3.W54A755 1995

To Anne and Geraldine

Table of Contents

Acknowledgements

The author thanks the following writers who helped with these poems: Anne M. Kelly, Marilyn Bowering, Anne Swannell, Derk Wynand, and Phyllis Webb.

Gratitude as well to the author's great-great-grandmother Elizabeth Harrison Harten, her daughter Matilda, her granddaughter Edith, and Lloyd, her great-grandson. They lived a long time and photographed well.

The draughts within her agéd house do fill
her ears like the breath of animate objects.

—Anna Wollis

Headstone

Below the fresh
rectangle of sod:

a form that will survive
even those chiselled letters
above it.

Already, the soil
gathers round the bones
like a higher order of flesh.

Equipment Failure

First the telephone
goes dead.

Then the wind
loses its murmuring tongue
in the eaves.

Fair-weather cloud
drops rain
like a ruptured bladder.

And the sun
not burning my eyes
though I stare at it.

And the angry figure
in wing-shaped splints,

bashing his trumpet,
blow by blow,
to dust.

Falling Landscape

A single snowflake
makes the load unbearable.

The wind blows its note
and the barn gives a moan
which bounces off hills
like a child's vast ball
so rapidly thrown
it becomes invisible.

An overhanging limb
lets its icicle go
through the space
where the roof has just been.

The elements
sweep away motes
rising from the split members.

Elemental

Hydrogen

How its passion
for attachment to neighbours
links us to its world.

There:
bonds with oxygen,
bonds with nitrogen.

Here:
water for faces,
ammonia for floors.

But we suspect
other possibilities.
Men whip around
though nobody's there.
Women in skirts recoil.

Helium

Inert.
Unreactive.
Colourless.

Its own indifference
the air that floats it away.

Lithium

This lightest of metals—

on wing, almost,
at the blacksmith's ear.

Use me, it whispers,
your horses will fly.

Carbon

Sleight-of-hand.
Deft shuffle of atoms,
each more unlikely,
more complex than the last.

But for its best trick,
listen . . .
(breathing).

Oxygen

The wrong word spoken
or spark
shot from a narrowed eye
preceding (barely)
conflagration.

Arsenic

An interest in what dances
not just in the wind.

How it slips
through back doors
into their parties

to eavesdrop,
to study their motion in pairs,
to slide a tart tongue into wine
that alters them so.

And when the last breaths
inside them fly out
and every guest stops
twitching on the floor—

Why? it cries
to an echoing room,
Why are their bodies so still?

Uranium
Heavy with electrons
which makes it unstable,
like a mother under stress,
who hits an obstacle
and bursts into tears.

Unnilpentium
Coached
toward
existence
in labs,
it reaches
for shape,
wavers,
and is
gone.

Carpenter

He even looks
like an old hammer:
hard shiny head
and lines like wood grain
on a thin neck—
years ago
pulling me out of myself
like a twisted nail.

I visit him
bearing a can
of his favourite tobacco.

He rolls a cigarette
with fingers
rough as sandpaper,
and though over 80
appraises me
with a plumb carpenter's eye.

Yes sir, he finally says.
Screw them in right once
and they last a lifetime.

Song of the Magi

An intolerable light came blazing
out, and in it was one whose grace
and whose beauty were greater than
the beauty of the world.
          —The Epic of Gilgamesh

to the land of twin rivers
        where the suns flashed
we bring these gifts

vials of barium
        rare selenium
                ionized gold

they shall protect her
        as she grows
from the wellspring of evil

she will walk unharmed
        through the storms
                of glowing rain

        and eat the
paste white berries
        without becoming sick

over her life dark ereshkigal
        shall have no range
                no power

                but shall rend
        her tangled hair
shedding tears like dust

the anunnaki shall spit
missiles of venom
but the venom shall slip from her

harmless as the crimson flies
on the plains
of asphodel

never will she
wander the wilderness
in search of the wind

but the wind at her beckon
shall nudge
her brightly mottled feet

she will sleep by day
at the mouth
of the rivers

the gulf's cry a restful tune
and at night
walk singing

through the reeds
crushing snakes
and poisonous toads

her long neck craning for rain
she will wander
free of disease

she will simulate time
she will live
forever

He

The use of the universal 'he' is now grammatically incorrect.
—Creative Writing Workshop Blackboard

Out-of-breath, *he* leaned against a noun.
Through the gaps between letters
reached jagged streaks of light
the pink of faded blood.
The blackboard was quiet,
except for the far-off staccato of hammering chalk.

It, neutral as always, puffed on a cigarette.
The pink light glittered on exhaled smoke particles.
"You're not a verb," *it* said, "you can't outrun them."
Though fatigued, *he* heaved his small chest defiantly out—
"I represent all, not half of mankind."
"Humankind," *it* corrected.
He winced, and laughed bitterly.
"Ah yes, how well I remember—"
Then *he* stopped—
the scene still too clear:

brutalized *-kind* tied to a table,
it male member gone,
its inner hyphen exposed like a ripped-loose organ,
and the hulking *human,* cold and sexless,
bending low . . .

He shivered as a chill breeze
from an unseen vent swept across the wordscape.
Among flaccid adjectival mounds
loomed the blockish forms of proper nouns.
Participles dangled loosely.
A lone interjection jabbed the air
with odd, explosive angles.
A ghostly copse of indefinite articles
wavered on the horizon.
And beyond: the border
of the blackboard, the metal rim, and freedom.

He watched the cigarette smoke curl over the noun.
The pinkish light seemed stronger.
The soprano of a distant police siren cut through the air.
He took *its* hand and squeezed.
It pressed limply back.
"Good-bye, *it*," said *he*.
"Good-bye, *he*," said *it*.

He brushed the chalk from his clumsy pronoun feet,
and ran.

Anguished Poet Seeks Self in Verse After Combing Countryside Without Success

I am here, somewhere, in this poem,
whatever I may mean, wherever here may be.

I am not there. I am here, right here,
here in this place I have come to.

Yet the where of this here evades
my dark-hued demeanour: who will find me,

all I have been, all I am, all I would be,
peering at myself, as if myself,

in this word-bleared mirror? Will I find me?
And if this, what will I see

when my quiver-lipped image returns my peer?
My step itself is a fog of ink

on this poem's echoing lines,
on the lines of this poem echoing.

But in which of all these murmuring pairs
am I? The very, very first of these?

Hunched nervously between the *here*
and *in* on the opening line?

Or maybe alone, just that, and shivering
on the second line, between

the *may* and *mean*, these both of them
suddenly small against the print-throttled page.

Or am I in the heart of the pair
I have not yet completely written?

Or the pair I am about to write?
Or the fair, far pair I may never write?

But which of these? Which?
The very one that follows here slow?

This drunken one, weary, bearded
with commas, stuttering, stuttering, on?

Or there, there, back there,
pairs and pairs and pairs and pairs ago.

Perhaps I shall suddenly appear
before the next *e* in *me*,

beneath the next *y* in *my*,
beside the singular *I* in *I*

that is alone and alone (and alone).
Perhaps I shall be spied

compressed below the loose-lipped *s* in *us*,
weighted down as I was, and I am,

and indeed I will most likely
be, by its troublesome plurality.

Or could it be I am nowhere among all these,
but lost, completely lost, forever lost in the vapid

white spaces between today and tomorrow
and the day after tomorrow,

washing now and always about the poem's sore knees
as it kneels, forever short,

of those greening glades, those shagging sheep,
it would come to.

Twenty-Four Poets' Haiku on the Colour Green

1. *Theodore Roethke*
On a dusty shelf
Pale green tendrils violate
Their cellophane bag.

2. *Galway Kinnell*
Buried laughter shakes
the stones and monuments of
graveyards turning green.

3. *Irving Layton*
Moist and steamy wings
flashing greenly in the fir—
blue ink swells my pen.

4. *Randall Jarrell*
A green tint growing
Over the prone soldier's face—
O treacherous spring!

5. *Anne Sexton*
Little green faces
twist round in the wind and grin
at me from the trees.

6. *Basil Bunting*
The green, sot! See it
(if your dim eyes can) singeing
the husks of the world.

7. *Derk Wynand*
The greenhorn's fingers:
seeking, meeting resistance;
the woman's face: red.

8. *Miroslav Holub*

orange yellow green
blue indigo violet
ultraviolet

9. *Charles Simic*

Newton grappling with
His formulae—the apple,
Green, gripping the branch.

10. *Robert Bly*

Repairman adjusts
the television (blood on
the news report green).

11. *e.e.cummings*

he looks and looks but
the plum refuses to be
anything but green

12. *Sylvia Plath*

We drown in forests.
The green waves do not see us—
Rolling, still rolling.

13. *John Ashbury*

The green cormorant
detaches it cummerbund
which keeps on dancing.

14. *Al Purdy*

God-awful, this mess!
Defacement by yahoos with
paint not even green.

15. *William Carlos Williams*
A parked chevrolet.
The green finish yellowing
in a harvest moon.

16. *Amy Lowell*
I shake by the flames—
Burning in your pale green eyes
Only the camp fire.

17. *Alden Nowlan*
Such greens! May they cap
my plate always: these goosetongues,
samphires, fiddleheads!

18. *Ted Hughes*
Greenery picked clean.
The burnt-out forest rattles
black bones in the wind.

19. *Donald Justice*
The weathered green door,
Cock-eyed on its single hinge,
Knocking in the wind.

20. *Muriel Rukeyser*
Which of us will sing
for green-ice lakes, frozen streams,
in their silent time?

21. *John Berryman*
The greengrocer scowls
& hits again Mr. Bones
with Mr. Prices.

22. *Eugène Guillevic*
It isn't you, green,
the painter chooses when he
thinks about dying.

23. *Wallace Stevens*
Green of memory
Flaming brighter in his mind
Than any landscape.

24. *Elizabeth Bishop*
The child's snowy hand
does not stir, even slightly,
though green sprigs are near.

Tale

One by one
small figures
emerge from the midnight wood.

At the border of a frozen lake
the leader sniffs the air,
scans the horizon for tall silhouettes.

The snap of settling ice
rifles the silence.

They hunch in the cold
to look smaller.
They break for the opposite shore.
Their boots send hairline cracks
through the crusty snow.

Splitting cloud uncovers the moon—
searchlight over a wall of hills
which tears from each figure
a shadow of human dimensions.

Hiroshima

When God was a boy,
he must have pulled wings
off angels.

The Moon

The moon is a pocked
and lifeless sphere
a quarter-million miles away.

Nevertheless,
the light it casts
is very brilliant, very white.

Some who study philosophy
consider it odd,
a paradox,

that a flawed and distant object
could shine so brightly,
so perfectly.

For astronomers, intent
on the nature of such light,
this causes no concern,

while lovers, intent
on each other,
give it little thought.

Isobars

We ignore
the long shadows
that crowd the window.

We write letters,
feed children,
go about our business.

But the trips
to other rooms
become more frequent.

We pad by mufflers
and overcoats
hanging on hooks.

The walls
of our bungalow crack
as the temperature falls.

Scene with Shirt

Sky ashen
from snow it has lost.

Below,
almost buried in drifts,
an abandoned farmhouse.

Attached is a clothesline
and shirt bleached white
by the years it's been
hanging there.

It flaps away flakes
with a tattered cuff,

twists in the wind
to clean shoulders,

then billows horizontally,
as if something cold
from the soil
was slipping it on.

Exercise

The nightly walks
round the graveyard
wore thin long ago.

This compulsion for exercise
that might have saved him once
is now an annoyance:

breezes that swirl
right through him
as if he's not there,

inscriptions in a tongue
he can no longer read,

lovers that shudder like flame
should he happen by.

His circuit's never over
too soon, as far
as he's concerned.

Only then can he lie
again with the earth,
and listen to the radio
of wind and rain in the trees.

Only then can he hear,
without feeling guilty,
the background static of worms
as they exercise.

Eraser

He moves up. Moves down.
And then pauses . . . unsure.
With each change of heart,
with each new opinion,
he wears away
another piece
of himself.

Poets Write Haiku on Office Stationary During Coffee Breaks

1

Telephones vibrate
as the oil furnace kicks in
automatically.

2

The dry leaves rustle
in the breeze of employees
hustling down the hall.

3

Proofreading copy,
his groan escapes the transom . . .
a typist flinches.

4

All morning she chews
the chocolate-covered nuts
he'd slipped in her drawer.

5

A new programmer
slips his bible between two
software manuals.

6

A tiny spider
adds a web to the mouth of
a styrofoam cup.

7

Two statisticians
talk standard deviation
at the urinals.

8

Typing letters is
easy once you get the hank . . .
Typing letters is

9

The water cooler
gurgles away as stenos
coddle the spigot.

10

Typist glances up
when the boss returns tousled—
fingers pat the keys.

11

The pigeon roosting
over the washroom window
drops a popcorn seed.

12

The secretary
adjusts her hairdo in the
display terminal.

13

How small the shoppers
and the unemployed appear
on sidewalks below.

14
High above, the sound
of plane engines as busy
pilots work the air.

15
Sun in the boardroom!
Security officer
quickly draws the blinds.

16
A service call made
when a villanelle prints out
on the fax machine.

17
He dictates curtly:
just seventeen syllables
per memorandum.

18
Window thrown open.
Pink slip, tearfully crumpled,
spirals to the street.

A Villanelle for All Saints' Day

The rubber mask looks like a half-formed face
On the little ghost out for Halloween.
And the broken clock says it's 12:06 a.m.

She opens the door, doesn't know how to say
That it's hours too late, there are no other treats.
The rubber mask looks like a half-formed face.

The ghost doesn't speak, holds the sack in her way
As she says, *Oh how strangely familiar you seem*
And the broken clock says it's 12:06 a.m.

She gathers from purses a fistful of change.
Drops it in, but the bag is a fathomless sea.
The rubber mask looks like a half-formed face.

How much more do you want me to pay?
Why are you staring? Why won't you leave?
And the broken clock says it's 12:06 a.m.

The tiny hands hold out the sack like a plate.
There's a ravenous hunger her silver can't feed
The rubber mask looks like a half-formed face.
And the broken clock says it's 12:06 a.m.

Suitcase

This is proper for a suitcase:
to sit empty in a corner

until needed,
for the leather halves

to part
at the tug of a zipper

and fill with the things
we give it.

These it carries,
working them,

shifting them
to its dimensions,

till we reach for it
in travel, and take back,

changed,
what we gave.

Antiques

Not taking her medication
taught objects to speak.

Each with a thought
now revealed it.

Each with a history
told it.

Amid the mad chatter
of household possessions,
her father
tries reading the paper.

He flings it away,
stomps to the staircase.
Take your damn pills!
he hollers.

She does, ending
the bedlam of things
with one swallow.

The tick of the clock
replaces its heartbeat.

Old portraits
sag on the wall.

Smoke rises mutely again
from her father's bone pipe.

Five Winter Cinquains

I

Under
glassy ice we
see a carp manoeuvre
torpidly through clouds and pallid
faces.

II

Clusters
of black skiers
widen and separate
as among them the white mountain
ascends.

III

Disguised
below a pair
of snowy epaulets,
the crow reconnoitres the moon
for food.

IV

Cold dog,
skilfully dead,
with four legs twisting up,
catches our unexpected lunge
of breath.

V

A chill
wind scuttles in
from the north and erases
two handprints in a tramped welter
of soles.

Non-Smoker

The unlit cigarette in her mouth.
The lit match in my hand.
The troublesome stretch of space
that separates them.

In the half-light
of restaurants
non-smokers have much
to consider:

proper angle to cock the wrist,
trajectory of the arm,
rate at which the match
devours itself . . .

The window behind her is open.
Curtains expand in the breeze.
Fingertips detect
the heat of the flame.

Gripping the match
like a miniature torch,
I enter that divide
of silence and draft.

Radio Waves

The electromagnetic spectrum is a vast sea
of radiation ranging from gamma rays to
the longest radio waves, colors we can never see.
—Michael A. Seeds, Foundations of Astronomy

1

Walls do not consider them.
They do not consider walls.
They pass through one another
without comment.

2

The dramas we know
only by hearsay.

The waves that slip
by barricades
and enter our rooms in force.

Their insistence in corners:
searching through dust,
curtains, paper—
finding at last those loops of wire
which shatter our sleep
with a radio's sudden blast.

3

Because they do not deafen us
like the waves of the air,

Because they do not crush us
like the waves of the earth,

Because they do not drown us
like the waves of the sea,

We let them sink, taut
with purpose, into our flesh.

4

The setting red sun.
The violet sky.
The spread of light we know well.

But what of
that sunset only hinted at
in the crackle of a dial?

5

Parabolic dishes
cocked upward like ears—

The cries as stars explode,
galaxies crash:

These agonies
that whiten the faces
of those who listen

Food

It is Monday.
I have overslept.
The mattress groans as I leap out of bed.
I arrive at work without breakfast.
By ten all I think of is food.
The secretary enters my office.
The mail rustles in her hand.
She drops it on my desk and leaves.
The top envelope is Neapolitan-striped.
The body of the letter spreads like batter.
Rows of boldface season the page.
I slip the edge of a sheet between my teeth.
No crumbs obscure the papery taste.
Wet ink fills the cracks in my tongue.
Heat rises from the vent.
The wall clock grumbles.
Air in the room slowly cooks.
The secretary returns to check my outbox.
Her dress is rice-paper thin.
Its white and green label shows through.
She steps back as I lean toward her.
I pick the berry-red buttons.
Snapped threads coil into curlicues.
The dress drops like cellophane.
Her lips round to the neck of a jar.
Mouthfuls of sound pour free.

Solitary Image

To the prisoner
at the bars of his cell,

to the bruised child
rocking by the bed grill,

to the woman leaning
from the steep bank
of the river—

the one lit window
with the figure in it
near the top of the skyscraper

gleams through the night
like the eye of a beast
scanning its territory.

Pi

This obsession
of circles.
This presence

between 3 and 4.
Even the way
it's pronounced
conveyes mixed feelings:

p spit out
like a bitter taste,
while *i* lingers

on the lips,
in the roundness
of the mouth,
as if the speaker senses

that the idea
has been dismissed
too soon . . .

Newton's Laws

1. $F=0 \Rightarrow v=const$
(A body moves with constant velocity
until acted on by an external force)

I am content,
with little interest in process,
the effort it requires.

Even my motions
are a kind of stillness.

Only another
can alter such dreamy paths.

2. $F = ma$
(Force equals mass times acceleration)

My indifference to velocity
confuses others.
They shake their heads
as if it makes no sense.

But I am subtle.
Only with change,
a slowing, or a kicking out,
do I jump, take note.

3. $F_{12} = -F_{21}$
(For every action there is an
equal and opposite reaction)

Is it fair to be called
obsessive just because
I answer every question,
respond to every touch?

Hearing a Knock

The middle of the night.
I wake to a knock.
Cold air brushes my skin
as I roll down the covers.

The stairway carpet
muffles each footfall.
I open the door
but no one is there.

It's too late to sleep.
I slip on my coat and go out
to watch a grey sky
filling with snow.

Fascist Haiku

I

Us and Them and Us.
How the sun flushes through
their vanishing faces.

II

We have sealed the trains.
On time, they spirit their freight
away from our towns.

III

My features the test—
I verify the hall mirror
reflects correctly.

IV

Bone heap in the field,
with its clean, compelling shape
and coloration.

V

Our leather boots are
spit-buffed to a painful shine.
Platz! Franzosenpack!

VI

Chestnut tree made blonde
by the glow the streetlight casts.
I salute, weave past.

VII

So much depends on
the brownshirts by the white truck
burning in the rain.

VIII

The flashes of light
in the circling hills remind
me of her necklace.

The Italian Campaign
Veteran Sobers Up

Carafes they had emptied
refilled by the light
as the mists
of the Riva degli Schiavoni
redden in the dawn,
then vaporize.

Weaving, he kicks
at the tight-lipped bottle
which rattles down
an embankment,
plopping bottom-up
in the dirty creek.

An early gondolier
cracks a seam
in the wine-coloured canal.
It ruffles like a sheet
to each smooth bank.

The bottle gurgles back
the brown water.
Bubbles struggle up
the narrow throat,
rupture in the air.

Through the window
of their room they watch
the sun's advance rays
mop up the late stars.
A runnel of light seeps down
the Spire of Palladio.

A canvas-back pickup
whips by.
The bottle-blonde inside
laughs at him.
The trailing corkscrew of dust
shears at his face.

The trucks start north.
The memory of her black hair
burns in the sun.
The soldier sitting beside him
passes the grappa.

Two crows coalesce
on a weather vane.
In the morning light,
lean houses, and peeling
Baptist paint.

Weather

The rain that plummets
to the roofs of houses,

the wind that pitches
like a heavy object
into trees,

the sleet that drops
the faces of men
and women hurrying by—

the freefall of turbulence.

He looks through the window,
bends with the storm.

Reaching for her coat,
she says,

It's not the weather,
it's the gravity—

fastening her high collar,
her smile, against
the good weather.

Particle Limericks

1

There was a neutrino from Kent,
who said, *Why pay any more rent?*
Without any mass,
not even an ass,
I might as well sit in a tent.

2

A drinking electron got tight,
charged randomly into the night,
with a sizzling sound,
he spun to the ground,
and threw up a bundle of light.

3

There was an unstable muon,
who realized something was wrong.
If I don't ditch some mass,
get rid of it fast . . .
But too late—the muon was gone.

Thirteen Ways of Looking at Pepper

"The Hendersons will dance and sing . . ."

1

Pepper-and-salt head
bends over a trumpet.
To the lonely city a dark bird calls.

2

The insubstantial help of friends:
the shadows of moths
peppering a dim spring.

3

Lucy lifts the final peppermint
from the box.
She slips it into her mouth
and chews thoughtfully.

4

Of the varied provisions
destined for cupboards,
only the dried berry
of the black pepper
will improve.

5

I was of many minds,
like a draft
which snatches grains of pepper.

6
Only the smokestacks to wish her well
as she carries the suitcase to the car.
The coal dust drops in her hair
like confetti.

7
The kite becomes a black dot—
marks the edge of the smallest
of many spheres.

8
Without warning, I sneeze
and startle from a dream.
Within the unlit kitchen
a pepper shaker rolls across the floor.

9
The abandoned food
grows stale on four plates.
Four beetles pick through the morsels,
avoid precisely the greying pepper.

10
Her little white book
is stamped
with small black faces.
They wince upon the open page
as snow clouds
paper the sky.

11
Nothing to say,
I pepper my scrambled eggs
and masticate.

12
The veteran dozes
in his sergeant's uniform.
Spotted fingers twitch
as the scratched record plays.
His breathing (contrapuntal)
accompanies the trumpeter
blowing the same notes over and over.

13
The family gathers round his bed.
He turns away,
and gazes at the endless fields
dark with peppergrass.

Windows

A girl in a sandalwood chair
faces the ocean.
Waves batter in
through a beachscape of rock.
Winds from China test the glass.

Inside a car.
Her face behind the window.
The wheels turn and the wheels turn
and scenery moves
in the still eyes.

Seated at the table.
Her daughter's voice beyond the panes
as a bass voice calls.
Lining her plate an assortment
of shapes to eat.

Standing in the quiet house.
The lines round her eyes
and the lines of the road
meeting at windows
impossibly clean.

Rocking chair
motionless in the umbra.
Parakeet's cry above the wind
as clouds part.
Cold stars sharp against glass.

Air Travel

the jolting seat
with a stranger at each elbow

the engine straining
   like an overworked furnace

the lift of this elevator
      without its building

the hour hand flung forward
         (or back)

the inverted sky
            with clouds below

the soft voice
               (almost musical)

whispering the altitude
                  in miles . . .